DayOne

HELP!

I STRUGGLE WITH ANXIETY

Phil Cottrell

Consulting Editor: Dr Jim Winter

© Day One Publications 2019
First printed 2019

ISBN 978-1-84625-669-1

Published by Day One Publications
Ryelands Road, Leominster, HR6 8NZ
Tel 01568 613 740
North America Toll Free 888 329 6630
email—sales@dayone.co.uk
website—www.dayone.co.uk

Printed by Orchard Press Cheltenham Ltd

CONTENTS

ENDORSEMENT

There are three reasons why this booklet is able to fulfil the author's stated desire to help others suffering with anxiety. Firstly, there are many who, while knowing Scripture's teaching 'to be anxious for nothing' or 'not to worry' nevertheless face a regular, wearying, often demoralizing, uphill battle with anxiety. Secondly, the author himself knows that struggle. His self-awareness and his sympathy for fellow strugglers will inspire confidence. Thirdly, he knows *where* to find peace, liberty and comfort *and* he knows *how* those things are found, gently persuading the sufferer to trust afresh in the loving heavenly Father revealed in Scripture.

Simon Clarke, one of the pastors,
Shepshed Word of Life Church

INTRODUCTION

Anxiety is something that many people struggle with today. It usually, though not always, goes hand in hand with depression. However, there is often a reluctance among us to admit to anxiety. Perhaps we think that speaking about feeling anxious will show our lack of spirituality, the smallness of our faith or our immaturity.

Yet Isaiah 12:2 says,

> *Surely God is my salvation;*
> *I will trust and not be afraid*
> *The LORD, the LORD, is my strength and*
> *my song;*
> *he has become my salvation.*

The 'trust' spoken of here is, of course, trust in our loving, gracious God. The more we are obedient and 'Cast all [our] anxiety on him because he cares for [us]' (1 Peter 5:7), the less of a problem our anxieties will be.

In an earlier book, *A Bruised Reed* (Evangelical Press, 2014), I wrote about my struggles with depression and my battles with associated anxiety. Then, in *Why Are You Downcast, O My Soul?* (Day One, 2017), I wrote solely about depression. In this short booklet I want to write about what anxiety has been like for me and how our Lord's grace has helped me to deal with it, in the hope that my experiences will help others.

The nature of fear

As with many of my dear brethren in the church, I am convinced that to be afraid, in and of itself, is not sinful. There are three reasons why I believe this to be so:

- Fear is part of our fallen condition.

- Fear can be unavoidable. For example: a fireman, trained in his profession, is called upon to enter a burning building to save someone. It would be strange indeed if there was not at least an element of fear in his mind.

- The sin associated with fear depends upon how we deal with, and respond to, our fear: wrong thinking can lead to sinful action or inaction. For example, Jesus has always been sinless. When he walked upon this earth, though tempted, he was always holy and pure. Yet faced with the agony of the cross, at Gethsemane he said, 'My soul is overwhelmed with sorrow to the point of death' (Matthew 26:38). Three times, with his face to the ground, he prayed, 'My Father, if it is possible, may this cup be taken from me. Yet not as I will, but as you will' (26:39). Surely, in his humanity, fear played a part in this prayer? (But let us never forget the outcome!)

Even the apostle Paul experienced anxiety. Nevertheless, he was helped in the first century by the same Lord of the twenty-first century: 'when we came into Macedonia, this body of ours had no rest, but we were harassed at every turn—conflicts on the outside, *fears within*.¹ But God, who comforts the downcast, comforted us by the coming of Titus' (2 Corinthians 7:5–6).

We see from Paul's words that, as the body of Christ, we *need* one another: '[Titus] told us about your longing for me, your deep sorrow, your ardent concern for me, so that my joy was greater than ever' (2 Corinthians 7:7). So let us be prepared, under our God's gracious hand, to share our anxieties with one another. We can then experience the joy that our

---

1   All emphasis in Scripture quotations has been added.

loving Father intends for us, even in the midst of our troubles.

One of the aspects concerning anxiety that I have to remind myself about is that I need to tell *my Father*. Prayer is not about method, technique or eloquence; it is about *a relationship*. My Lord knows all my thoughts. He knows my anxieties. He understands how I feel. But I need to tell him. I have found that giving over to him—rather than holding on to—my anxious thoughts, whatever they may be, brings real liberty and release to my heart. And in our prayers, let us remember the great treasure that we have to help us—the Bible.

> *For we do not have a high priest who is unable to sympathise with our weaknesses, but we have one who has been tempted in every way, just as we are—yet was without sin. Let us then approach the throne of grace with confidence, so that we may receive mercy and find grace to help us in our time of need.*
> (Hebrews 4:15–16)

The origin of fear

When a Christian becomes anxious, where does that fear come from? Our God is holy and wise, loving and kind. He did not create man, in his own image, to be fearful: 'So God created man in his own image, in the image of God he created him; male and female he created them.' (Genesis 1:27). Man was perfect, the pinnacle of his creation: 'God saw all that he had made, and it was very good' (1:31).

So what spoiled God's perfect creation of man? The answer is, of course, the Fall. When Adam and Eve disobeyed God, the entrance of sin corrupted everything for them. As sin became part of their nature, fear became part of their experience: 'Then the man and his wife heard the sound of the LORD God as he was walking in the garden in the cool of the day, *and they hid from the LORD God* among the trees of the garden' (3:8).

Only through repentance and faith in the Lord Jesus Christ and his perfect sacrifice for our sins can peace be restored between God and man. Christians are his children, born of the Holy Spirit. But that sinful nature of Adam will be with us until we are again made perfect when Jesus returns: 'For the sinful nature desires what is contrary to the Spirit, and the Spirit what is contrary to the sinful nature. They are in conflict with each other, so that you do not do what you want' (Galatians 5:17).

Does that mean we are *bound* by our sinful natures? Paul explains that we are not: 'You, however, are controlled not by the sinful nature but by the Spirit, if the Spirit of God lives in you. And if anyone does not have the Spirit of Christ, he does not belong to Christ' (Romans 8:9).

So what does this mean in practice in relation to my fears? I suggest this:

When fears arise within me, I need not be overcome by them. I can honour my risen Saviour through being obedient to his Word:

> *Trust in the LORD with all your heart*
> *   and lean not on your own understanding;*
> *in all your ways acknowledge him,*
> *   and he will make your paths straight.*
> *   (Proverbs 3:5–6)*

When my thinking gets caught up in how I see a situation and I get fearful, freedom from this fear comes from entrusting my mind into the hands of my loving Father and his promises. He knows everything that is going on; he will lovingly 'watch over [my] coming and going' (Psalm 121:8).

As I mentioned in Chapter 1, I am convinced that being anxious in and of itself is not sinful. 'The acts of the sinful nature are obvious: sexual immorality, impurity and debauchery; idolatry and witchcraft; hatred, discord, jealousy, fits of rage, selfish ambition, dissensions, factions and envy; drunkenness, orgies, and the like' (Galatians 5:19–21). Did you notice that being fearful is *not* included in this list? It is how we deal with our fears that can lead to sin. The alternative to giving way to our fears, and so sinning through action or inaction, is to submit to Christ's wonderful Spirit in us: 'But the fruit of the Spirit is love, joy, peace, patience, kindness, goodness, faithfulness, gentleness and self-control' (5:22–23). We bring praise and honour to our Lord by exhibiting these beautiful characteristics.

Our Father knows

For I am the LORD, your God,
who takes hold of your right hand
and says to you, Do not fear;
I will help you.

(Isaiah 41:13)

Why does God say, 'Do not fear'? Surely it is because he knows we tend to be fearful and he desires to deliver us from it. The phrase 'takes hold' speaks of the intimacy of a loving Father with his child and of a Father who will protect his child. David wrote, 'The LORD is close to the broken-hearted and saves those who are crushed in spirit' (Psalm 34:18). This speaks of the outpouring of our Father's love for those in deep sorrow, but perhaps David is also writing about those crushed by fear or overwhelmed by anxiety. *If so, our God has promised to save them.*

There are times when I become anxious because I face a frightening situation, but far more often my anxiety stems from timidity—a mind that does not reason as it should and so allows fearful thoughts to develop. At such times of anxiety the blessing I need is *peace*.

Far more than the absence of war or conflict, 'peace' in the Scriptures means a deep calm, a sense of well-being; the well-being that comes from a heart and mind assured of the love of God.

Through his Spirit, Jesus has given us *his* peace, a peace greater, deeper and more real than anything this world can give: 'Peace I leave with you; my peace I give you. I do not give to you as the world gives. Do not let your hearts be troubled and do not be afraid' (John 14:27). The peace of our Lord Jesus Christ is not something that I can earn or merit, it is his free gift, lovingly bestowed upon an undeserving sinner. Looking to him, trusting him, I must not allow my thoughts to unsettle me or make me afraid and by so doing compromise his wonderful gift.

Jesus' gift of peace is personal, since he knows me as an individual and cares for me as such. But he also cares for his church and desires for all his people to know his peace *together*: 'Let the peace of Christ rule in your hearts, since as members of one body you were called to peace. And be thankful' (Colossians 3:15). As I mentioned in Chapter 1, we are the body of Christ, and we need one another. What a wonderful thing to be 'called to peace'! And what a wonderful thing to give thanks for it!

Have you ever imagined your loving Father gently whispering to you, coaxing you, with the question, 'Can you not trust me?'

'Elijah was afraid and ran for his life' (1 Kings 19:3). Jezebel had threatened him, and the great man of God had only her murderous message of hatred before his eyes. Later on, having been comforted by the Lord, Elijah reached Mount Horeb. Then God spoke: 'The LORD said, "Go out and stand on the mountain in the presence of the LORD, for the LORD is about to pass by"' (19:11). There was a tremendous wind, then an earthquake, and then a fire. Almighty God, Creator of heaven and earth, showed his power. But then something astonishing happened: 'after the fire came a gentle whisper. When Elijah heard it, he pulled his cloak over his face and went out and stood at the mouth of the cave' (19:12–13).

Our God made his presence felt to his servant in great tenderness—the tenderness of a gentle voice, speaking as a loving Father. And in the Bible our Lord speaks to us in words of love to dispel our fears.

Do not worry

Worrying is a person's mind doing battle *with itself* in a futile attempt to overcome a seemingly insurmountable circumstance by mere thought alone. So when the dreaded problem persists, or comes about, what do we find? We find that the person's attempt to find peace about a situation through worrying *simply does not work*: 'Who of you by worrying can add a single hour to his life?' (Matthew 6:27).

It seems to me as a Christian that if I worry I am in essence 'playing God'. By worrying I am denying Jesus his rightful place as Lord. I am disregarding his command 'Cast all your anxiety on him because he cares for you' (1 Peter 5:7). I am basically saying that, in this situation, right now, about *this* matter, I do not believe Jesus really cares.

Many years ago, at times when I became really anxious, I suffered from panic attacks. Prior to suffering them myself I thought they were absurd;

to my shame, I would even be scornful when I saw a person having a panic attack. But I can assure you that they are dreadful. How grateful I am to my loving, gracious God that over time he has delivered me from them. And the cure is a mind sufficiently strengthened by right thinking concerning the character of our God. He does not leave me to 'sink or swim'. He *does* care.

In dealing with the subject of worry, our Lord gently reasons with us. He does not want our God-given minds to be burdened with fear. I have found Jesus' teaching on worry in Matthew 6, part of the Sermon on the Mount, to be a great blessing:

- 'Look at the birds of the air; they do not sow or reap or store away in barns, and yet your heavenly Father feeds them. Are you not much more valuable than they?' (6:26). He feeds the birds, so can you doubt that he will also feed you?

- 'And why do you worry about clothes? See how the lilies of the field grow. They do not labour or spin. Yet I tell you that not even Solomon in all his splendour was dressed like one of these' (vv. 28–29). Our Father's care for us knows no limit. His giving out of his gracious heart is *extravagant*.

- 'So do not worry, saying, "What shall we eat?" or "What shall we drink?" or "What shall we wear?" For the pagans run after all these things, and your heavenly Father knows that you need them. *But seek first* his kingdom and his righteousness, and all these things will be given to you as well' (vv. 31–33). Confident that our Lord will provide our daily needs, our minds should be *preoccupied* with faithfully serving him. And all that he graciously gives to us *is given for this purpose*.

- 'Therefore do not worry about tomorrow, for tomorrow will worry about itself. Each day has enough trouble of its own' (v. 34). This verse really strikes a chord with me. I find it so foolishly easy to attempt to sort out future problems today! Yet how often we arrive at the 'crisis' day to find that things are not at all as difficult as we expected and even that the trouble has evaporated! We need to bear in mind that our Lord gives us grace *when we need it*.

So do not fear, for I am with you;
do not be dismayed, for I am your God.
I will strengthen you and help you;
I will uphold you with my righteous
right hand.

(Isaiah 41:10)

Our Lord is with us every day, and every hour of every day. Let us entrust our future to his care.

As for God, his way is perfect;
the word of the LORD is flawless.
He is a shield
for all who take refuge in him.
For who is God besides the LORD?
And who is the Rock except our God?
It is God who arms me with strength
and makes my way perfect.
He makes my feet like the feet of a deer;
he enables me to stand on the heights.

(Psalm 18:30–33)

What a wonderful promise of God's peace is given to us in the words: 'Do not be anxious about anything, but in everything, by prayer and petition, with thanksgiving, present your requests to God. And the peace of God, which transcends all understanding, will guard your hearts and your minds in Christ Jesus' (Philippians 4:6–7). This is a promise of a peace beyond our understanding, but amazingly real. The promise is conditional, of course, upon our obedience.

When I get anxious about something, quite often I find myself thinking, 'Why are you getting anxious about *this*? This is a ridiculous thing to worry about; you are being silly.' If you are like me, what you are being anxious about may indeed seem absurd. But we each need to accept that the cause of our anxiety is real to us and therefore we must deal with it as our loving Father bids us do here.

One question we need to ask ourselves often is: 'What are my desires?' The cause of my anxieties may well be that I have lost my spiritual focus. Paul writes, 'Since, then, you have been raised with Christ, set your hearts on things above, where Christ is seated at the right hand of God. Set your minds on things above, not on earthly things' (Colossians 3:1–2). If my mind is centred upon how to please my Lord, my worries—worries that are of self-interest—will disappear like the morning mist.

Fear of man

Fear of other people can influence us in ways that affect our faithfulness to the Lord and lead us into sin. We can, for example, be intimidated by the sheer aggressiveness of a person. Some people can make us feel inadequate, and feeling self-conscious is by no means a small thing for some. Feeling timid can be a difficult thing to overcome at times.

Fear of man is the fear of what another person thinks of us. It is the sense of powerlessness that can be so paralysing; whilst in its grip, you are no longer in control of your life.

The way to be free of such anxiety is to have a mind that is centred upon our Saviour. *He* is Lord, and our lives belong to *him*. 'Therefore, holy brothers, who share in the heavenly calling, fix your thoughts on Jesus, the apostle and high priest whom we confess. ... Christ is faithful as a son over God's house. And we are his house, if we hold on to our courage and the hope of which we boast' (Hebrews 3:1, 6). No one can separate us from our Lord Jesus Christ. That person or group of people who make us fearful are subject to God's will, whether they believe it or not:

> *I make known the end from the beginning,*
>   *from ancient times, what is still to come.*
> *I say: My purpose will stand,*
>   *and I will do all that I please.*
> *From the east I summon a bird of prey;*
>   *from a far-off land, a man to fulfil my*
>   *purpose.*
> *What I have said, that will I bring about;*
>   *what I have planned, that will I do.*
>   *(Isaiah 46:10–11)*

Whatever attitude a person has towards me and whatever that may lead that person to say or do, I am loved eternally by the Lord Jesus Christ. He is sovereign over his world. 'For by him all things were created: things in heaven and on earth, visible and invisible, whether thrones or powers or rulers or authorities; all things were created by him and *for him*' (Colossians 1:16).

Christian organizations tell us there is more persecution today of our brothers and sisters worldwide than ever before. In the UK, on the whole, we are free to worship and serve our Lord. But even here, there is strife within families, arrests of open-air preachers, unbiblical laws and sanctions against expressing one's faith in the media.

Persecution of God's people was also present 2,000 years ago. In response, the apostles prayed for boldness: 'Herod and Pontius Pilate met together with the Gentiles and the people of Israel in this city to conspire against your holy servant Jesus, whom you anointed. They did what your power and will had decided beforehand should happen. Now, Lord, consider their threats and enable your servants to speak your word with great boldness' (Acts 4:27–29). They knew that the gospel of our Lord Jesus Christ needed to be proclaimed. And it still needs to be proclaimed in the UK today. We too need to ask our Lord for grace to be fearless.

Whenever a person makes us fearful we need to remember that it is our Lord's view of us that matters. He understands how we feel and his name is honoured when our overriding desire is to please him.

Fear of death

Death brings home the reality of life like nothing else does. As time passes, the scenes of life change constantly: different shades of colour, lighter, darker, happier, sadder. But then approaches an event never seen before, like a figure in the shadows we know is there but do not recognize.

Even for a Christian, I believe that fear of death is natural. Experience cannot help us. Reason cannot help us. No one can say, 'I know what you are facing—I have been there' in order to offer sympathy. How, then, do we dispel this fear?

The answer must lie in the words spoken so tenderly by our Lord Jesus Christ to Martha: 'I am the resurrection and the life. He who believes in me will live, even though he dies; and whoever lives and believes in me will never die' (John 11:25–26). It is the presence of our Saviour which gives us peace: 'Even though I walk through the valley of the shadow of death, I will fear no evil, *for you are with me*' (Psalm

23:4). Jesus also said, 'My sheep listen to my voice; I know them, and they follow me. I give them *eternal* life, and they shall never perish; no one can snatch them out of my hand' (John 10:27–28).

The definition of 'eternal' is 'without beginning or end, unchanged by time':

- 'He [God the Father] chose us in him [Christ] before the creation of the world' (Ephesians 1:4)—we have *always* been Christ's.

- 'Of the increase of his [Christ's] government and peace there will be no end' (Isaiah 9:7)—Christ's peaceful lordship over us will never cease.

- 'Jesus Christ is the same yesterday and today and for ever' (Hebrews 13:8)—Christ will not change, and after we are called home we will not change either.

All our Lord's people are secure for ever in his hands. Our God is faithful, his Word is true, his promises never fail. This is our future:

For the Lord himself will come down from heaven, with a loud command, with the voice

> *of the archangel and with the trumpet call*
> *of God, and the dead in Christ will rise first.*
> *After that, we who are still alive and are left*
> *will be caught up together with them in the*
> *clouds to meet the Lord in the air. And so*
> *we will be with the Lord for ever. Therefore*
> *encourage each other with these words.*
> (*1 Thessalonians 4:16–18*)

About three years ago the thought of death troubled me persistently over several weeks. I did not understand why then, nor do I understand now. I had thoughts like 'Is my soul really going to live for ever?' and 'When I die, what will the passage from this life be like?' Fear lurked in the back of my mind.

But then, sometime later, I was suddenly admitted to hospital to undergo tests for heart problems. For two days the possibility of death was real, at least to me. I know that my brothers and sisters in the Lord were praying for me. And throughout my week in hospital, in a calm and peaceful state of mind, my thought was 'Even if I die, all will be well. I belong to Jesus and I will always be with him.' The reality of that truth is given by God the Holy Spirit. And it is given in grace, I believe, *when the reality of that truth is needed*. I am convinced that when a brother or sister faces death, my experience will be theirs. 'Never will I leave you; never will I forsake you' (Hebrews 13:5; cf. Deuteronomy 31:6).

I quoted earlier from John 11:25–26: 'I am the resurrection and the life ... whoever lives and believes in me will never die.' I deliberately omitted the end of verse 26: 'Do you believe this?' As with Martha, you and I must believe our Lord. Then we will be unafraid, and all will be well.

Psalm 33

What if, like me, you are prone to anxiety by temperament, as if you perceive impending catastrophe at every turn? The struggle with anxiety can be relentless for some Christians, as each new day is seen as a time when new dangers emerge.

The following three psalms have been especially enriching to my heart and mind in my walk with our Lord.

Psalms 121 and 103

Psalm 121 affirms a loving God's care for me: 'The LORD watches over you' (v. 5). Psalm 103 is a 'request-free' psalm which I wrote about in *A Bruised Reed*. It speaks wonderfully of a Father's grace to a sinner like me:

> *He will not always accuse,*
> *nor will he harbour his anger for ever;*

he does not treat us as our sins deserve
or repay us according to our iniquities.

(vv. 9–10)

Psalm 33

I have also been greatly helped by Psalm 33. It shows me that the Father of our Lord Jesus Christ is Sovereign over all things. Each and every event, and each and every person in time and space, is subject to his will. With such a God as this, why should I be afraid?

Here are some verses from Psalm 33 for us to consider and reasons to praise him as we embrace these truths about his character:

- 'For the word of the LORD is right and true; he is faithful in all he does' (v. 4). He will never let me down.

- 'The LORD loves righteousness and justice; the earth is full of his unfailing love' (v. 5). His love, seen clearly only by eyes opened by his Spirit, is evident all around me.

- 'By the word of the LORD were the heavens made, their starry host by the breath of his mouth' (v. 6). Millions of stars have been gathered together in beautiful galaxies, more than man can number, all according to God's will.

- 'Let all the earth fear the LORD; let all the people of the world revere him. For he spoke, and it came to be; he commanded, and it stood firm' (vv. 8–9). All the wonders of nature were made at the sound of his voice. He simply declared his will and it was so.

- 'The LORD foils the plans of the nations; he thwarts the purposes of the peoples. But the plans of the LORD stand firm for ever, the purposes of his heart through all generations' (vv. 10–11). Nobody can prevent the plans of our Father from coming to pass, and that includes his loving purposes for me.

  Nowhere do we see 'the purposes of his heart' being fulfilled in the midst of sinful men more clearly than at Calvary: 'This man was handed over to you by God's set purpose and foreknowledge; and you, with the help of wicked men, put him to death by nailing him to the cross' (Acts 2:23). Wonderfully, it is also in the 'purposes' of God that we serve and worship a risen Saviour: 'But God raised him from the dead, freeing him from the agony of death, because it was impossible for death to keep its hold on him' (2:24). Jesus is Lord!

• No one on the face of the earth is outside the sovereign will of the One who 'From heaven ... looks down and sees all mankind', the one who 'from his dwelling-place ... watches all who live on earth' (vv. 13–14). We have been brought into a relationship with the living God who 'forms the hearts of all, who considers everything they do' (v. 15).

There is a mystery here. There are tyrants, evildoers, people who persecute the church and people who harbour unspeakable malice. But despite their freedom to choose such evil behaviour, their hearts are known to Almighty God and are subject to his will.

Praise God there is another mystery— the mystery of hearts formed by mercy and redemption: 'For we are God's workmanship, created in Christ Jesus to do good works, which God prepared in advance for us to do' (Ephesians 2:10). When I am struggling with anxiety and the days ahead are uncertain, the sovereignty of our Lord that I see in Psalm 33 is a great comfort to me, and meditating upon it often leads me to this verse in Ephesians.

- 'The eyes of the LORD are on those who fear him, on those whose hope is in his unfailing love' (v. 18). Our Father's love abides with his children—it is a love that never diminishes. If I place my life into his hands, day by day, I can have assurance that his love will *never* fail me, and I can know deliverance from anxiety.

- 'In him our hearts rejoice' (v. 21). Why? 'For we trust in his holy name.' There's that word 'trust' again. And when I start to get anxious, my God can say to me, 'Will you not trust me?' We can all rejoice in such a God as ours.

- 'May your unfailing love rest upon us, O LORD, even as we put our hope in you' (v. 22). This is the only request in the psalm. But I view it rather as an affirmation of our Father's unfailing love for you and for me. The God we see in this psalm is one who will never disappoint us all our days.

In *A Bruised Reed* I quoted from Isaiah 50:10: 'Let him who walks in the dark, who has no light, trust in the name of the LORD and rely on his God.' Notwithstanding the wonderful treasure we have of God's Word, the assurance of his Spirit and the help of brothers and sisters in Christ, there are times when we are perplexed, unsure and doubtful. Is this not the reality of life? I see echoes of this verse from Isaiah in Psalm 33. I can be anxious *or* I can trust in my Lord and rely upon him.

Self-forgetfulness

What is it that makes me anxious? As discussed in the previous chapters, I get anxious when:

- I am disobedient to my Lord—and my conscience reminds me that 'Your eyes are too pure to look on evil; you cannot tolerate wrong' (Habakkuk 1:13).

- I rely upon myself—and not 'on God, who raises the dead' (2 Corinthians 1:9).

- I worry about what people may think of me— and do not have my eyes fixed on the Lord, remembering that 'Fear of man will prove to be a snare' (Proverbs 29:25).

- I get preoccupied with my scarce resources of energy, time and money—and fail to answer the question, 'He who did not spare his own Son, but gave him up for us all—how will he not also, along with him, graciously give us all things?' (Romans 8:32).

- I fret about what might happen in the future—and don't keep in mind that 'The LORD is faithful to all his promises and loving towards all he has made' (Psalm 145:13).

With the exception of the first point above—that is, a wilful action that I know to be wrong—the causes of my anxiety all seem to originate from the sinful nature with which I was born, a nature from which I will not be free until I pass from this present life.

So should I just shrug my shoulders and say, 'That's just the way I am'? No; the Scripture quotations show that none of us are *compelled* to be anxious. As with depression, we can address it and not be ruled by it. And also as with depression, I think a key element in dealing with our anxieties is self-forgetfulness.

It is so easy for our minds to become self-centred: 'What do *I* want?' 'This is *my* opinion.' 'How will this affect *me*?' I can easily forget to pray about the needs of others, but I have no problem remembering *my* needs!

What does a servant do? He gives his time and abilities to meet the needs of his master. In the case of Christians, that 'Master' is the Lord Jesus Christ. We are those 'who have been chosen according to the foreknowledge of God the Father, through the sanctifying work of the Spirit, for obedience to Jesus Christ and sprinkling by his blood' (1 Peter 1:2). Our minds should, therefore, be taken up with how best we can serve the One who saved us: 'You are not your own; you were bought at a price' (1 Corinthians 6:19–20).

There are people in need all around me, people whom God loves and whom God has called me to help in any way I can. Do I constantly think of how I can do this? Their greatest need is to hear the gospel of the Lord Jesus Christ. Do I think about how I can help with this?

We are part of the family of God, his church. Do I think about the needs of my brothers and sisters in Christ and how I can meet their needs?

> *Then the righteous will answer him, 'Lord, when did we see you hungry and feed you, or thirsty and give you something to drink? When did we see you a stranger and invite you in, or needing clothes and clothe you?*

*When did we see you sick or in prison and go
to visit you?' The King will reply, 'I tell you
the truth, whatever you did for one of the
least of these brothers of mine, you did for me.'*
(Matthew 25:37–40)

Being anxious can easily distract us from what we are meant to do on this earth—to serve our risen Saviour. May we all look forward with confidence to the day of our Lord's return and hear him say, 'Well done, good and faithful servant! You have been faithful with a few things; I will put you in charge of many things. Come and share your master's happiness!' (Matthew 25:21, 23).

A fear we need

Having considered our Lord's exhortations not to fear, it may seem rather strange to now consider something we *do* need to fear. The difference, of course, is in where that fear is directed. To fear God is fundamentally different from other fears.

I have found the doctrine to 'fear God' a struggle to understand, but I believe it means a deep reverence for God based on knowledge of his character.

The model prayer Jesus gave us begins with the words 'Our Father in heaven, hallowed be your name' (Matthew 6:9). To 'hallow' God means to have a profound awareness, in our hearts and minds, of his awesome holiness. The seraphs called to one another, 'Holy, holy, holy is the LORD Almighty; the whole earth is full of his glory' (Isaiah 6:3). John writes, 'This is the message we have heard from him and declare to you: God is light; in him there is no darkness at all' (1 John 1:5). It is because of the utter sinfulness of man, in contrast to the absolute holiness of God, that

Jesus died on the cross—the Lamb of God, a perfect sacrifice for our sins. Jesus 'rescues us from the coming wrath' (1 Thessalonians 1:10).

A real consciousness of God, which comes only through his Spirit, brings with it a sense of awe. God is God, and man is man. Here are three Scripture passages to help us:

> *'To whom will you compare me?*
> *Or who is my equal?' says the Holy One.*
> *'Lift your eyes and look to the heavens:*
> *Who created all these?'*
> *(Isaiah 40:25–26)*

> *This is what the LORD says:*
> *'Heaven is my throne,*
> *and the earth is my footstool.*
> *Where is the house you will build for me?'*
> *(Isaiah 66:1)*

> *'For my thoughts are not your thoughts,*
> *neither are your ways my ways,'*
> *declares the LORD.*
> *'As the heavens are higher than the earth,*

> *so are my ways higher than your ways*
> *and my thoughts than your thoughts.'*
> (Isaiah 55:8–9)

Psalm 34: 9 says, 'Fear the LORD, you his saints, for those who fear him lack nothing.' What an astounding declaration is attached here to the command to fear God! It must be a command of prime importance if what follows obedience to it is so great.

We sometimes get anxious about how to deal with what lies ahead for us in life. But here are two more wonderful promises associated with fearing God:

> *Who, then, is the man that fears the LORD?*
> *He will instruct him in the way chosen*
> *for him. ...*
> *The LORD confides in those who fear him.*
> (Psalm 25:12, 14)

Fearing God brings with it great blessing.

Fear of God is to be a characteristic of those who serve the risen Lord Jesus Christ. *But how are we to do this in practice?* David tells us:

> *Come, my children, listen to me;*
> *I will teach you the fear of the LORD.*

Whoever of you loves life
  and desires to see many good days,
keep your tongue from evil
  and your lips from speaking lies.
Turn from evil and do good;
  seek peace and pursue it.

(Psalm 34:11–14)

'Keep your tongue from evil and your lips from speaking lies.' How hard it can be to control our words! By the grace of God, we should desire to say only what is good and pure. I want to praise and honour my Lord and be a real blessing to people. James tells us, 'If anyone is never at fault in what he says, he is a perfect man, able to keep his whole body in check' (James 3:2). 'Turn from evil and do good.' We have a choice: each day that our Father gives to us we can choose to be disobedient to him, or we can be faithful.

'Seek peace and pursue it.' This reminds us that peace is not something that comes naturally, not even for God's people. 'The heart is deceitful above all things and beyond cure. Who can understand it?' (Jeremiah 17:9). Our *natural* inclination is sinfulness and a turning away from God. But, thanks to his grace and the enabling of the Holy Spirit, we *can* serve our Lord faithfully, bringing pleasure to his heart.

I think this verse is striking and most instructive. The peace of God doesn't just 'happen'; we have to search it out and keep on after it. We must be diligent in our walk with the Lord—in prayer, in meditation on the Bible, in attentiveness to faithful preaching and in the help from other Christians. Our God is faithful, and if we are sensitive to the leading of the Holy Spirit, he will help us.

So many people in our world today seem to live in a state of anxiety. If we are truly God-fearing, living in deep reverence and awe of God, what a testimony that will be to a watching world! Our fear of God and the peace it instils in us will itself speak of the life-transforming power of the gospel of our Lord Jesus Christ.

A final word

As we noted at the start, anxiety and depression usually go hand in hand. Whilst it may not be possible for some Christians to live free from them entirely, I am convinced we can live free from their dominance.

My prayer and hope is that those troubled by anxiety may all be able to say, 'I will trust and not be afraid. The LORD, the LORD, is my strength and my song; he has become my salvation' (Isaiah 12:2).

Likewise, my prayer and hope is that those troubled by depression may be able to say, 'Why are you downcast, O my soul? Why so disturbed within me? Put your hope in God, for I will yet praise him, my Saviour and my God' (Psalm 42:5; 43:5).

The verse quoted above from Isaiah speaks of 'my song'. The psalmist in the verse above says, 'I will yet praise him.' Anxiety and depression come from our thoughts, and these affect how we feel. But I have found that praising and thanking our

Lord helps me enormously in dissipating anxiety and depression.

But here is the paradox. If our *motivation* for praising and thanking our Father is to feel good, we fail in our understanding of him and we will not receive the blessing we desire. The fear of God instils *worship*. And worship is to be from the heart, a *giving* of oneself to our Lord and not a desire to *receive* from him.

So let us truly worship our Lord and leave the blessing in his hands. Earlier we considered Psalm 33:

> *Sing joyfully to the LORD, you righteous;*
> *it is fitting for the upright to praise him.*
> *Praise the LORD with the harp;*
> *make music to him on the ten-stringed lyre.*
> *Sing to him a new song;*
> *play skilfully, and shout for joy.*
>
> (33:1–3)

I can think of no better reason to worship our God, who heals our anxiety and depression, than the one that is given to us in verses 4 and 5 of the psalm:

> *For the word of the LORD is right and true;*
> *he is faithful in all he does.*

The LORD loves righteousness and justice;
the earth is full of his unfailing love.

Where can I get further help?

I have been helped by the following three hymns. Reflecting on the words with the melody in my head is a real comfort.

- 'Immortal, Invisible, God Only Wise' (Walter Chalmers Smith, 1824–1908). This hymn draws my thoughts away from myself and towards the character of our great God, who is sovereign over all events.

- 'A Debtor to Mercy Alone' (Augustus Montague Toplady, 1740–1778). This hymn reminds me that my life is in the hands of our merciful God and that I am secure in him, now and for ever.

- 'Be Still, My Soul: The Lord Is On Your Side' (Katharina von Schlegal, b. 1697; tr. Jane Laurie Borthwick, 1813–1897). This is my favourite hymn. It speaks honestly and eloquently about the trials and sorrows of life, and yet gently reassures me that my God is ever faithful to bring me through them.

Booklets in the *Help!* series include …